Thinking Critically:
Illegal Immigration

Other titles in the *Thinking Critically* series include:

Thinking Critically:
Illegal Immigration

Jim Gallagher

ReferencePoint
Press®

San Diego, CA

For more information, contact:
ReferencePoint Press, Inc.
PO Box 27779
San Diego, CA 92198
www.ReferencePointPress.com

Picture Credits:
Cover: vichinterlang/iStockphoto.com
All charts and graphs by Maury Aaseng

LIBRARY OF CONGRESS CATALOGING-IN-PUBLICATION DATA

Name: Gallagher, Jim, 1969– author.
Title: Thinking Critically: Illegal Immigration/by Jim Gallagher.
Other titles: Illegal Immigration
Description: San Diego, CA: ReferencePoint Press, Inc., 2019. | Series: Thinking Critically series |
    Audience: Grade 9 to 12. | Includes bibliographical references and index.
Identifiers: LCCN 2018038621 (print) | LCCN 2018046096 (ebook) | ISBN 9781682825389 (eBook)
    | ISBN 9781682825372 (hardback)
Subjects: LCSH: Illegal aliens–United States–Juvenile literature.
Classification: LCC JV6483 (ebook) | LCC JV6483 .G36 2019 (print) | DDC 364.1/370973—dc23
LC record available at https://lccn.loc.gov/2018038621

Contents

Foreword

"Literacy is the most basic currency of the knowledge economy we're living in today." Barack Obama (at the time a senator from Illinois) spoke these words during a 2005 speech before the American Library Association. One question raised by this statement is: What does it mean to be a literate person in the twenty-first century?

E.D. Hirsch Jr., author of *Cultural Literacy: What Every American Needs to Know*, answers the question this way: "To be culturally literate is to possess the basic information needed to thrive in the modern world. The breadth of the information is great, extending over the major domains of human activity from sports to science."

But literacy in the twenty-first century goes beyond the accumulation of knowledge gained through study and experience and expanded over time. Now more than ever literacy requires the ability to sift through and evaluate vast amounts of information and, as the authors of the Common Core State Standards state, to "demonstrate the cogent reasoning and use of evidence that is essential to both private deliberation and responsible citizenship in a democratic republic."

The *Thinking Critically* series challenges students to become discerning readers, to think independently, and to engage and develop their skills as critical thinkers. Through a narrative-driven, pro/con format, the series introduces students to the complex issues that dominate public discourse—topics such as gun control and violence, social networking, and medical marijuana. Each chapter revolves around a single, pointed question such as Can Stronger Gun Control Measures Prevent Mass Shootings?, or Does Social Networking Benefit Society?, or Should Medical Marijuana Be Legalized? This inquiry-based approach introduces student researchers to core issues and concerns on a given topic. Each chapter includes one part that argues the affirmative and one part that argues the negative—all written by a single author. With the single-author format the predominant arguments for and against an issue can be synthesized into clear, accessible discussions supported by details and evidence including relevant facts, direct quotes, current examples, and statistical illustrations. All volumes include focus questions to guide students as they read each pro/con discussion, a list of key facts, and an annotated list of related organizations and websites for conducting further research.

The authors of the Common Core State Standards have set out the particular qualities that a literate person in the twenty-first century must have. These include the ability to think independently, establish a base of knowledge across a wide range of subjects, engage in open-minded but discerning reading and listening, know how to use and evaluate evidence, and appreciate and understand diverse perspectives. The new *Thinking Critically* series supports these goals by providing a solid introduction to the study of pro/con issues.

Illegal Immigration

The United States is often called a nation of immigrants—a place where people of different nationalities and backgrounds can come to find a better life. Some immigrants come seeking greater economic opportunities; others are fleeing political violence or religious persecution. Whatever their reasons for coming, US laws require immigrants to receive permission from the government before they can enter the United States.

Since the mid-1960s, when Congress passed the current laws that regulate immigration, more than 59 million immigrants have come to the United States legally. But millions of other foreigners are also living in the United States without permission of the US government. These people are often called illegal immigrants, undocumented immigrants, or unauthorized immigrants.

There is no way to know exactly how many illegal immigrants are living in the United States. Statistical analysis of population surveys indicate that the illegal immigrant population is between 10 million and 14 million. The most commonly accepted demographic data is from the Pew Research Center, which in 2017 estimated that there were about 11.3 million people living in the United States illegally. The center estimated that about 8.1 million of these illegal immigrants were working in the United States. They make up about 5 percent of the total US workforce and are employed mostly in agriculture or construction. Almost 60 percent of the undocumented immigrant population live in six states: California, Texas, Florida, New York, New Jersey, and Illinois.

Why They Come

Illegal immigrants tend to live in the shadows. They cannot obtain a US Permanent Resident Card, or "green card," which would authorize them to live and work in the United States. Nor are they eligible for Social Security, health care programs, and certain other government-provided benefits. Despite the drawbacks to illegal immigration, many people still do it. Most come for financial reasons. Even low-skill minimum-wage jobs in the United States pay up to three times as much as the daily wage illegal workers could earn in their home countries. More money usually translates to a better life for them, their children, and even family members back home.

Other illegal immigrants hope to find safety and freedom in the United States. Some come from countries that are torn by civil wars, troubled by violent gangs or drug cartels, or ruled by repressive regimes. To these individuals, the relative safety and freedom of life in America—even for someone who is here illegally—is worth the risk.

It is likely that some illegal immigrants tried to follow the legal route. But it is hard for foreigners to immigrate legally. The United States only grants immigration visas to a small percentage of those who apply each year. Those who do not receive a visa are put on a waiting list—but some wait decades for a visa. As of 2018, approximately 1.26 million Mexicans were on the waiting list for immigrant visas, according to the US Department of State. Millions of people from other countries are also waiting to obtain immigrant visas.

How They Come

At one time, the most common way immigrants entered the United States illegally was to sneak across the border with Mexico—perhaps by cutting through a wire fence, climbing over a wall, trekking through a desert, or swimming across a river. Since the early 2000s, however, additional security on the southern border has greatly reduced the number of illegal crossings that succeed.

Today many undocumented immigrants originally entered the United States legally under nonimmigrant visas, then remained in the country

9

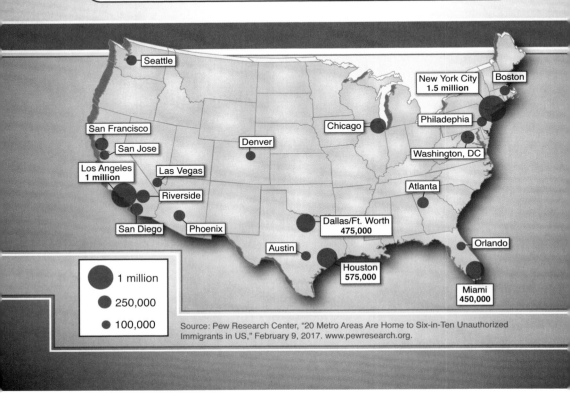

20 Metropolitan Areas with the Largest Number of Unauthorized Immigrants

Seattle

New York City
1.5 million

Boston

San Francisco

Chicago

Philadephia

San Jose

Denver

Washington, DC

Los Angeles
1 million

Las Vegas

Atlanta

Riverside

San Diego

Phoenix

Dallas/Ft. Worth
475,000

Orlando

Austin

Houston
575,000

Miami
450,000

● 1 million

● 250,000

● 100,000

Source: Pew Research Center, "20 Metro Areas Are Home to Six-in-Ten Unauthorized Immigrants in US," February 9, 2017. www.pewresearch.org.

after their visas expired. Some may have entered as tourists, students, or seasonal workers but decided not to leave when their visa term ended.

A 2017 report by the Center for Migration Studies found that from 2007 to 2014, about 66 percent of illegal immigrants had originally entered the United States with a valid visa and remained beyond their period of admission. The center's study found that these visa overstayers had exceeded illegal crossers in every year since 2007. The study's authors note, "This trend in increasing percentages of visa overstays will likely continue into the foreseeable future."[1] Today it is estimated that overstayers account for more than 40 percent of the total undocumented immigrant population.

Problems and Solutions

The long-term presence of undocumented immigrants in the United States has created a variety of complicated family situations. For example, under the US Constitution, any child born in the United States is automatically granted citizenship. However, this does not confer any right to citizenship or permanent resident status to the infant's parents. As a result, millions of children who are American citizens live with one or more parents who have no legal right to be in the United States and face deportation if they are discovered.

By the same token, individuals who are living illegally in the United States cannot apply for permanent residence, even if they marry a US citizen. Thus, there are hundreds of thousands of Americans whose spouses are undocumented and therefore subject to deportation.

Another issue is that some illegal immigrants brought their young children with them when they sneaked into America. Most of those children probably did not realize they were living in the United States illegally until they applied for a driver's license or sought to enroll in college and were denied because they did not have a green card or other proper documentation.

> "This trend in increasing percentages of visa overstays will likely continue into the foreseeable future."[1]
>
> —Center for Migration Studies

To help these young people, legislation like the Development, Relief, and Education for Alien Minors (DREAM) Act has been introduced in every session of Congress since 2001. The DREAM Act would provide a pathway to legal status for undocumented youth who were brought to this country as children (often called "Dreamers" in the media). The most recent variation of the DREAM Act, introduced in the Senate in July 2017, would give 3.4 million undocumented high school graduates a three-step pathway to US citizenship through college, work, or service in the military. As of the fall of 2018, Congress had not acted on this proposed law.

While president, Barack Obama encouraged Congress to reform immigration laws and deal with the illegal immigrant population. When

Congress failed to act, Obama issued an executive order called Deferred Action for Childhood Arrivals (DACA) in 2012. This program protected some of the Dreamers from deportation. Two years later, in November 2014, Obama proposed another program that would have protected from deportation the undocumented immigrant parents of Dreamers. In response to a court challenge, that program (Deferred Action for Parents of Americans and Lawful Permanent Residents, or DAPA) was blocked by a federal judge. It was then rescinded in June 2017 by the new US president, Donald Trump.

The Trump Effect

During his 2016 presidential campaign, Trump promised strong measures to curb illegal immigration: construction of a higher wall along the southern border and zero tolerance for criminal aliens. Six months after rescinding the DAPA order, Trump announced that DACA protection would expire in March 2018. Like Obama, Trump also encouraged Congress to resolve the nation's immigration issues.

Trump also promised to end what he called the "catch-and-release" policies of the Obama administration, in which people who requested asylum after being caught trying to cross the border were released into the United States until a court hearing. (Asylum is protection offered to foreigners who are being persecuted in their home countries.) Because of a high backlog of cases, these hearings could not be scheduled for a year or more, during which time many immigrants were allowed to live freely in the United States. Under Trump's new policy, anyone caught crossing the border illegally—including those who claimed to be seeking asylum—would face criminal prosecution.

This hard-line policy caused an outcry after it was implemented in the spring of 2018, when major media outlets began reporting that thousands of children and their parents had been separated from each other after being caught trying to cross the border. Administration officials explained that families caught crossing the border could only be detained for twenty days. After this, adults were charged with "illegal entry," a misdemeanor, and transferred into the criminal justice system. Because the children could not accompany their parents into federal prison, they were classified as "unaccompanied minors." By law, they were placed in the custody of another federal agency. In response to widespread criticism, on June 20, 2018, Trump ordered this policy to be ended.

Illegal immigration remains one of the most controversial and divisive issues today. There is strong disagreement among Americans about whether the presence of illegal immigrants helps or hurts US workers and over whether these immigrants receive more in government benefits than they generate through economic activity and the payment of taxes. Experts, activists, and government leaders disagree about whether a border wall would be the most cost-effective way to prevent future illicit crossings. And both Republicans and Democrats recognize that something must be done about the 11.3 million illegal immigrants living in the country, although there is no consensus over whether that should involve a path to citizenship, mass deportation, or some other option. Clearly, questions like these will continue to be asked until solutions are found.

Chapter One

Does Illegal Immigration Hurt US Workers?

Illegal Immigration Hurts US Workers

- Illegal immigrants take jobs from less-educated Americans and depress wages for those jobs.
- Businesses benefit from hiring illegal workers, but workers lose out.
- Taxes paid by American workers subsidize public assistance for native-born workers who have lost jobs to illegal immigrants.

The Debate at a Glance

Illegal Immigration Does Not Hurt US Workers

- Illegal immigrants help the US economy by taking low-skill jobs that Americans do not want.
- In states with more undocumented workers, skilled workers tend to make more money, and the economy's overall productivity increases.
- Illegal immigrants spend a high percentage of the money they earn, which helps the overall economy.

Illegal Immigration Hurts US Workers

"Immigration has a negative effect on workers without a college degree. That's especially true in agriculture and construction. . . . In those industries, immigration lowers wages and drives out native-born workers."

—Kimberly Amadeo, journalist

Kimberly Amadeo, "Immigration's Effect on the Economy and You," Balance, September 11, 2018. www.thebalance.com.

Consider these questions as you read:

1. Do you think the US government has a responsibility to ensure that all Americans have opportunities to work? Why or why not?
2. In your opinion, is it a problem that illegal immigrants often have to work in unsafe or unsanitary conditions that most American workers would not tolerate? Explain your answer.
3. How persuasive is the argument that allowing illegal immigrants to work imposes a hidden cost on society? Explain your reasoning.

Editor's note: The discussion that follows presents common arguments made in support of this perspective, reinforced by facts, quotes, and examples taken from various sources.

In his January 2018 State of the Union address to Congress, Donald Trump spoke about the impact of illegal immigration. He complained that the relaxed policies of previous administrations had "allowed millions of low-wage workers to compete for jobs and wages against the poorest Americans."[2]

Many economists and experts agree with this assertion by the president. A *New York Times Magazine* article summarizes years of research on this topic, reporting, "Labor economists have concluded that undocumented workers have lowered the wages of U.S. adults without a high-school diploma—25 million of them—by anywhere between 0.4 to 7.4 percent."[3]

The Poorest Workers Are Displaced

Pro-immigration advocates often claim that illegal immigrants only take jobs that Americans do not want. This is simply not true—the United States does not have a huge labor shortage that requires the import of millions of low-wage unskilled workers from other countries. There are already millions of unemployed American workers who could fill those jobs if given the opportunity.

The unemployment rate tends to be highest among Americans who did not complete high school. In 2017, the most recent year for which accurate data is available, the Bureau of Labor Statistics reported that the unemployment rate among American workers who had not earned a high school diploma was 7.7 percent—considerably higher than the unemployment rate among high school graduates (5.3 percent) or college graduates (2.5 percent). The unemployment rate was much higher among African Americans who had not completed high school, at around 18 percent.

The presence of millions of illegal workers, most of whom do not have a high school education or training in the sort of vocational or technical skills that are valuable in a modern economy, means more competition for low-skill jobs. In this environment, businesses can offer lower wages because they know that there are many people who need work and have few other options. African American high school dropouts, a group that already struggles to get jobs and earn a living wage, suffer most.

> "Labor economists have concluded that undocumented workers have lowered the wages of U.S. adults without a high-school diploma—25 million of them—by anywhere between 0.4 to 7.4 percent."[3]
>
> —*New York Times Magazine*

Lax Immigration Enforcement Encourages Hiring of Cheap Labor

Since 1986, it has been against the law for companies to knowingly hire illegal immigrants. However, the federal government has made only a token effort to enforce the law. Since 2009, Immigration and Customs Enforcement (ICE) officials have only inspected the I-9 employment eligibility records of a tiny fraction of the roughly 28 million businesses in the United States. The extremely low possibility of being caught encourages businesses to hire illegal immigrants, who will work cheaply, instead of native-born workers or legal immigrants.

I-9 Employment Eligibility Inspections

Fiscal Year	Form I-9 Inspections (Audits)
2009	1,444
2010	2,196
2011	2,496
2012	3,004
2013	3,127
2014	1,320
2015	1,242
2016	1,279
2017	1,360

Source: Laura D. Francis, "ICE Work-Site Enforcement Likely to Borrow from Obama, Bush," Bloomberg News, February 5, 2018. www.bna.com.

This situation is further complicated by illegal workers who are willing to put up with poor or dangerous working conditions. American laws are in place to keep workplaces safe and ensure that workers are treated fairly. Illegal immigrants may not know about such laws. Or they may be so grateful for jobs in the American economy that they will put up with unsafe workplaces in order to work. In the process, they wind up displacing low-skilled American workers because the Americans refuse to work under these conditions.

It is also easier for some businesses to exploit illegal workers. Business owners know they can pay low wages or not pay overtime because the workers are afraid that if they complain about mistreatment, someone from the government will find out about their illegal status. A 2016 investigation by the *Boston Globe* found numerous cases of workers who were injured on the job or who were not paid the wages they were promised for their work. "These workers, eager for a paycheck, are often paid below the prevailing wage and illegally, in cash," notes the *Boston Globe* report. "They are also the most likely to be subjected to unsafe work conditions, without insurance to cover medical bills or lost pay if they get hurt. And the unscrupulous contractors who employ them are too seldom caught and penalized."[4]

Businesses Take Advantage of Workers

American businesses are the ones that benefit from illegal immigration, at the expense of native-born workers. Companies can save money by paying illegal immigrants lower wages. They also eliminate the expense of providing health or retirement benefits that American workers would expect. This amounts to an enormous transfer of wealth from workers to businesses and large corporations. In 2016 testimony to the US Senate Subcommittee on Immigration and the National Interest, Harvard economist Dr. George J. Borjas estimated that the practice of hiring immigrant workers redistributes some $565 billion a year from workers to American businesses.

Federal law forbids American companies from hiring illegal immigrants. Employers must ensure that each of their workers provides documents (such as a Social Security card or green card) that indicate their eligibility to work in the United States. Companies are supposed to keep I-9 forms for each worker on file and present them for inspection by immigration officials, if and when requested. Violations of the law can result in fines of between $250 and $2,000 for each illegal worker hired.

However, government inspections of I-9 records are relatively rare. And because the law requires proof that the employer "knowingly" hired the illegal worker, violators often get off with no consequences or just a token punishment. "It is generally felt that these civil penalties are too low and enforced too infrequently to have much, if any, deterrent effect on employers," notes Heritage Foundation scholar Robert Rector. "Many employers simply treat the possibility of a small fine as a normal, minor cost of doing business."[5]

A Flawed System

The US Department of Homeland Security, which is responsible for protecting the border and for immigration and customs enforcement, offers an online database program called E-Verify that is supposed to help businesses quickly confirm whether a prospective worker is eligible for employment in the United States. However, most businesses are not required by law to use the system, so they do not. As of 2018, only about 4 percent of the more than 18 million businesses in the United States participated in the E-Verify program.

Experts agree that when it comes to preventing illegal immigrants from working, the federal government system appears far more effective than it really is. "Nobody wants to shut down businesses," comments Alex Nowrasteh, an immigration policy analyst at the Cato Institute's Center for Global Liberty and Prosperity. "That's expensive politically and economically. It's much easier to have a system that doesn't work [but which] sounds like a silver bullet."[6]

> "Many employers simply treat the possibility of a small fine as a normal, minor cost of doing business."[5]
>
> —Heritage Foundation scholar Robert Rector

Another way large employers get around the rules is by subcontracting work to much smaller firms that employ illegal immigrants. This way the employer is not responsible for vetting the workers—and not on the hook if there is a government audit of worker documentation. Often, these smaller companies only exist to provide services such as janitorial work or food preparation to the larger corporation. If there is an audit, the company will dissolve. Later, a new one that serves the same function can be formed.

Indirect, Unseen Costs

When an illegal immigrant takes a job that would otherwise have gone to a low-skilled American worker, there is an indirect, unseen cost in the form of government assistance. This expense is borne by all American workers who pay taxes. Without a job, a low-skilled American worker is more likely to enroll in a government welfare program. High school dropouts—the workers most likely to be displaced by illegal immigrants—make up around 25 percent to 30 percent of welfare recipients, according to data from the US Department of Health and Human Services. Taxpayers wind up supporting these workers to the tune of $360 billion a year.

Additionally, low-skilled Americans are much more likely to turn to criminal activities if they cannot find a job. Nearly 80 percent of the inmates in state and federal prisons do not have a high school diploma. Most of these prisoners are African American. The federal and state governments spend billions each year on criminal justice and the prison system. If it were not for illegal immigrants filling so many of the available low-skill jobs, millions of these citizens might have found legitimate employment. The resulting high cost of the justice system hurts all taxpaying American workers.

The evidence is clear that turning a blind eye toward illegal immigration hurts American workers. The least-educated workers are impacted the most, but all taxpayers pay a price when illegal workers disrupt the labor supply. Unfortunately, while the system allows illegal immigrants to work, it also creates the conditions for them to be exploited by business owners. It is a system that has to be changed in fairness to all workers.

Illegal Immigration Does Not Hurt US Workers

"If we lose the workers who are here illegally, it's hard to see how they'll be replaced, because Americans are reluctant to take these jobs, particularly the ones harvesting crops."

—Tamar Haspel, *Washington Post* columnist

Tamar Haspel, "Illegal Immigrants Help Fuel U.S. Farms. Does Affordable Produce Depend on Them?," *Washington Post*, March 17, 2017. www.washingtonpost.com.

Consider these questions as you read:

1. If you needed work and were offered a job as a farmworker, would you take it? Why or why not?
2. Do you agree with the claim that low-skilled illegal workers complement, rather than compete with, other workers in fields like construction and food service? Explain.
3. How persuasive is the argument that undocumented workers have only a small effect on the wages of American workers? Explain your answer.

Editor's note: The discussion that follows presents common arguments made in support of this perspective, reinforced by facts, quotes, and examples taken from various sources.

Imagine a bowl of fresh fruit on your table. If it was grown in the United States, chances are an undocumented immigrant picked the fruit for you. According to the most recent National Agricultural Workers Survey, published by the US Department of Labor in 2016, undocumented workers make up nearly half (47 percent) of the American agricultural workforce. Although machines harvest produce such as wheat, soybeans, and corn, farmers still rely heavily on individual workers when it comes to fruits and vegetables that are easily bruised or damaged. Planting, cultivating, and harvesting these crops often involves grueling physical labor.

According to a 2017 *Washington Post* report, the typical migrant farmworker's day begins around 3:00 a.m. The workers spend ten to fourteen hours picking fruit like strawberries, cherries, or apples or cutting vegetables like broccoli, asparagus, or celery. The work involves constant bending and stooping or climbing tall ladders. There are few breaks for food or water, even on the hottest days. The pay rate can be $12 an hour or more, but because the work is seasonal and a job is not guaranteed each day, many migrant farmworkers only earn around $10,000 a year.

> **"You don't need a deep analysis to understand why farm work wouldn't be attractive to young Americans."[7]**
>
> —Philip Martin, economist and agriculture expert at the University of California–Davis

Over the past few years, farms have had to increase hourly wages and even offer health care and other benefits because of a shortage of workers willing to put in the long, hard hours needed to harvest food. Yet farmers from California to Michigan to Georgia report that millions of tons of produce was left unpicked in American fields in 2017 and 2018 because they could not find enough farmworkers to harvest the crops.

Americans Will Not Do This Work

Even for people with little education or job skills, there are much easier ways to make a living than farmwork. Over the past three decades, the data shows that few Americans have been willing to take farm jobs, even when they are desperate. A 1996 US Department of Labor report found that only about five hundred American workers applied for over ten thousand available farm jobs that year. The situation has not changed. "I don't think anybody would dispute that that's roughly the way it is now," Philip Martin, an economist and agriculture expert at the University of California–Davis, told the *Los Angeles Times* in 2017. "You don't need a deep analysis to understand why farm work wouldn't be attractive to young Americans."[7]

A recent North Carolina case study illustrates how unlikely Americans are to engage in farmwork. In 2011 the North Carolina Growers Association, a statewide organization of farmers, listed sixty-five hundred available jobs. According to state data, there were 489,000 unemployed workers in the state. Most of the jobs were located in areas of the state where the unemployment rate was 10 percent or more. Only 268 Americans applied for one of the farmworker jobs, and 245 were hired. The rest of the jobs were filled by foreign farmworkers, most of whom came from Mexico. One-third of the American workers did not even show up for their first day of the season. Of the 163 North Carolina workers who did start the season, only 7 were left at the end. By contrast, about 90 percent of the Mexican farmworkers completed the season. The study's author, Michael A. Clemens, concludes:

> The data show this is not a case of farmers preferring foreign labor because they can pay foreign workers less; no matter how bad the economy turned, there were still very few native workers who were willing to take farm jobs. The picture is clear: farms will not get the labor they need from natives alone. Without foreign seasonal workers, whole subsectors of agriculture would not exist in North Carolina today.[8]

Complement, Not Compete

Not only are undocumented immigrants not taking jobs away from American workers, they are helping Americans earn more than they would otherwise. Research conducted by University of California–Davis economist Giovanni Peri has found that undocumented workers tend to complement other workers. For example, a construction company may employ undocumented workers to help more skilled tradespeople on the job site. With the undocumented workers carrying tools or building materials and cleaning up the job site, the skilled laborers do not become bogged down in basic tasks. They can focus on quickly completing tasks they are trained to do and moving on to the next task. This greater efficiency lowers the overall cost of construction and increases the number

Undocumented Workers Play a Vital Role in the US Economy

Undocumented immigrants make up only about 5 percent of the US workforce, but they are vitally important in farming, construction, and the service industry (which includes domestic help). In farming alone, they make up more than half of the hired labor. Those industries depend heavily on undocumented workers largely because the jobs they offer are low-paying, physically demanding, and unappealing to US citizens. By taking jobs that Americans do not want, illegal immigrants in no way hurt American workers, but they do play a vital role in supporting the US economy.

What Unauthorized Workers Do

Hired farmers	53%
Construction	15%
Production	9%
Services	9%
Transportation	6%
Overall workforce	5%

Source: Mary Jo Dudley, "These US Industries Can't Work Without Illegal Immigrants," CBS News, June 25, 2018. www.cbsnews.com.

of jobs that the company can accept, thus increasing its profitability. The same effect is found in other fields in which undocumented immigrants often work, such as food service, hospitality, or landscaping.

Peri found that the economy in states with more undocumented immigrants grew because skilled workers earned more money and worked more hours. He determined that undocumented workers increased legal workers' pay in complementary jobs by up to 10 percent. "My studies . . . show that, in fact, native and immigrant workers do take different jobs, do have some different skills, and do specialize in different productive tasks," Peri told an interviewer in 2018. "And this reduces direct competition. If you account for that, you get a very small impact—or no impact—[on wages] for those at the lowest levels of education."[9]

In a paper published by the National Bureau of Economic Research, Peri and a coauthor suggest that if the unauthorized worker population declined, the effect on American workers would be mixed. Unskilled American workers might see a small increase in wages, but higher-skilled American workers could see declines in both wage and employment rates.

Other experts agree with these findings. "Research shows that low-skilled immigration has at most a small effect on the wages of native-born workers," writes Noah Smith, a professor of finance at Stony Brook University. "Since refugees tend to be very low-skilled immigrants, these findings imply that illegal immigration to the U.S. didn't put many—or any—native-born Americans out of work."[10]

Paying Their Way

The evidence indicates that the American economy needs immigrant workers in order to function most efficiently. If the entire undocumented workforce were to be deported, the US economy would suffer. It is estimated that there are about 8.1 million undocumented workers, which represents roughly 5 percent of the total American labor force. An analysis by the American Action Forum determined that mass deportation could reduce the value of the country's annual economic production by $1.6 trillion, or around 8.5 percent.

> "Research shows that low-skilled immigration has at most a small effect on the wages of native-born workers."[10]
>
> —Noah Smith, professor of finance at Stony Brook University

The state of Arizona provides an example of what happens when undocumented immigrants are driven out of the workforce. In 2007 the Legal Arizona Workers Act required employers to use the federal E-Verify system to check the legal status of potential employees. In 2010, Arizona SB 1070 gave police broad power to detain undocumented immigrants. Passage of these two laws resulted in more than 40 percent of Arizona's undocumented immigrant population leaving the state over the next few years. This resulted in a steady economic decline: Without enough workers, Arizona's gross domestic product dropped by an average of 2 percent every year from 2008 to 2015.

The negative effect of losing undocumented workers would not be felt only by the farms or construction companies that employ them. A program of mass deportation, as some in the Trump administration have proposed, would result in the loss of billions of dollars that undocumented workers spend each year in their communities on vehicles and fuel, food, housing, health care, and entertainment. These are goods and services provided by American businesses. Losing that revenue could mean these businesses can employ fewer Americans and local and state governments would see a decline in revenues from sales taxes.

It would be foolish and short-sighted to try to drive undocumented immigrants out of the workforce. Like it or not, their labor plays a vital role in the US economy.

Chapter Two

Does Illegal Immigration Strain Public Services?

Illegal Immigration Does Not Strain Public Services

- Illegal immigrants are not eligible for most federal assistance programs.
- Although illegal immigrants are not eligible for most federal assistance programs, the taxes they pay help fund those programs.
- Fear of deportation keeps many illegal immigrants from seeking government benefits for eligible family members.

The Debate at a Glance

Illegal Immigration Strains Public Services

- School districts often must implement expensive programs to properly educate the children of illegal immigrants.
- Most illegal immigrants do not have health insurance, so the cost of their emergency medical care is borne by American taxpayers.
- Studies show that the federal, state, and local governments spend much more on services for illegal immigrants than they receive from them in tax payments.

Illegal Immigration Does Not Strain Public Services

"Despite scapegoating in public discourse, the drain that undocumented immigrants place on government benefit programs is small. The number of low-income undocumented immigrants is small relative to the size of the overall low-income population, and federal law restricts their participation in most programs."

—Tara Watson, professor of economics at Williams College

Tara Watson, "Do Undocumented Immigrants Overuse Government Benefits?," EconoFact, March 28, 2017. https://econofact.org.

Consider these questions as you read:

1. In your opinion, are concerns about undocumented immigrants receiving government assistance exaggerated? Why or why not?
2. Do you believe it is fair that undocumented immigrants who pay taxes cannot benefit from certain government programs? Why or why not?
3. In your opinion, is it a problem that undocumented immigrants who are eligible for certain government services do not seek those services? Why or why not?

Editor's note: The discussion that follows presents common arguments made in support of this perspective, reinforced by facts, quotes, and examples taken from various sources.

Donald Trump's first television campaign advertisement of the 2016 presidential election season claimed that if his opponent, Hillary Clinton, were elected, the system would stay "rigged against Americans. . . . Illegal immigrants convicted of committing crimes get to stay. Collecting Social Security benefits, skipping the line. Our border open. It's more of the same, but worse."[11]

Such claims are popular among many Americans who supported Trump's campaign—but they are not true. Websites that examine the claims that politicians and political organizations make in their public speeches and advertisements all agreed that Trump's statements about illegal immigrants receiving Social Security payments were false.

Nevertheless, false claims like this have often been used to argue that undocumented immigrants place an unfair strain on the services that the federal, state, and local governments provide. However, many studies have indicated that the actual financial impact of undocumented immigrants on public services is quite low and may be offset by other benefits that immigrants provide to the American economy.

Not Eligible for Many Programs

The federal government provides a variety of social insurance programs that are meant to help Americans. One of these, Social Security, pays monthly benefits to retired and disabled workers. Another, Medicare, provides health insurance coverage to Americans over age sixty-four and to anyone who receives Social Security disability payments. In 2018 around 67 million Americans received Social Security benefits, and 59 million received Medicare benefits.

US citizens are eligible for Social Security and Medicare. So are legal immigrants who meet certain criteria. However, undocumented immigrants are not eligible to participate in either of these programs.

Another commonly heard but false claim is that undocumented immigrants receive financial assistance through government welfare programs. The term *welfare* is generally used to refer to a variety of federal and state government programs that are intended to help the poorest Americans. One such program, commonly known as "food stamps," provides funding that low-income people can use to buy healthy food. Other welfare programs provide housing subsidies, benefits for disabled people, and health care. However, under federal law, undocumented immigrants are not eligible for any of these programs. "One of the most effective ploys by those attempting to vilify undocumented immigrants is to assert that those immigrants are stealing benefits from Americans," notes Robert A. Stribley in a *Huffington Post* essay. "Donald Trump has deployed this falsehood on multiple occasions both in his speeches and on Twitter long before becoming president. It's an insinuation quite divorced from reality."[12] In fact, as Stribley and many others have noted, taxes paid by undocumented immigrant workers help fund these programs, even though the workers cannot benefit from them.

Providing Financial Support

Funding for Social Security, Medicare, and the various welfare programs comes from federal taxes that are withheld from the paychecks of American workers. As of 2018 about 162 million Americans paid federal taxes toward the Social Security and Medicare programs. Among these taxpayers are roughly 4 million to 5 million undocumented immigrants.

This is nothing new. In 2013 the US Chamber of Commerce found that "more than half of undocumented immigrants have federal and state income, Social Security, and Medicare taxes automatically deducted from their paychecks."[13] Four years later, in 2017, the Institute on Taxation and Economic Policy wrote that "undocumented immigrants contribute significantly to state and local taxes, collectively paying an estimated $11.74 billion a year."[14] That figure includes more than $7 billion in state or local sales taxes, $3.6 billion in property taxes, and $1.1 billion in personal income taxes.

> "One of the most effective ploys by those attempting to vilify undocumented immigrants is to assert that those immigrants are stealing benefits from Americans. . . . It's an insinuation quite divorced from reality."[12]
>
> —Writer Robert A. Stribley

Some of that tax revenue goes toward funding Social Security, Medicare, and other federal programs. A Social Security Administration (SSA) report indicates that payroll contributions based on earnings by undocumented immigrants total about $12 billion a year. Roughly half of this figure is money withheld from the immigrant workers' paychecks; the other half represents a tax contribution paid into Social Security by their employer.

State and Local Taxes Paid by Undocumented Immigrants

According to a 2017 report by the nonpartisan Institute on Taxation and Economic Policy, undocumented immigrants pay about $11.74 billion in state and local taxes each year. This total includes more than $7 billion in sales taxes, $3.6 billion in property taxes, and $1.1 billion in income taxes.

State	Current State and Local Taxes	State	Current State and Local Taxes
Alabama	$62,312,000	Montana	$548,000
Alaska	$4,043,000	Nebraska	$39,800,000
Arizona	$213,574,000	Nevada	$86,101,000
Arkansas	$62,767,000	New Hampshire	$7,236,000
California	$3,199,394,000	New Jersey	$587,415,000
Colorado	$139,524,000	New Mexico	$67,743,000
Connecticut	$124,701,000	New York	$1,102,323,000
Delaware	$13,532,000	North Carolina	$277,402,000
Dist. of Col.	$31,765,000	North Dakota	$2,844,000
Florida	$598,678,000	Ohio	$83,247,000
Georgia	$351,718,000	Oklahoma	$84,765,000
Hawaii	$32,343,000	Oregon	$80,775,000
Idaho	$28,613,000	Pennsylvania	$134,872,000
Illinois	$758,881,000	Rhode Island	$31,154,000
Indiana	$92,200,000	South Carolina	$67,753,000
Iowa	$36,728,000	South Dakota	$5,338,000
Kansas	$67,843,000	Tennesee	$107,465,000
Kentucky	$36,629,000	Texas	$1,560,896,000
Louisiana	$67,991,000	Utah	$69,770,000
Maine	$4,367,000	Vermont	$2,936,000
Maryland	$332,248,000	Virginia	$255,965,000
Massachusetts	$184,605,000	Washington	$316,624,000
Michigan	$86,692,000	West Virginia	$5,112,000
Minnesota	$83,192,000	Wisconsin	$71,792,000
Mississippi	$22,684,000	Wyoming	$4,165,000
Missouri	$48,897,000	All States	$11,739,961,000

Source: Lisa Christensen Gee et al., "Undocumented Immigrants State and Local Tax Contributions," Institute on Taxation and Economic Policy, March 2017. https://itep.org.

These tax payments help fund social insurance and welfare programs, even though the immigrants themselves are not eligible to receive any benefits.

In effect, the contributions of undocumented immigrants subsidize these programs, allowing American citizens and eligible immigrants to pay less for the benefits that they receive. "Our projections suggest that the presence of unauthorized workers in the United States has, on average, a positive effect on the financial status of the Social Security program,"[15] write the authors of the SSA report.

Less Likely to Seek Help

In general, undocumented immigrants tend to keep a low profile, often out of fear that they might be identified and deported. As a result, undocumented immigrants are less likely than either legal immigrants or American citizens to apply for federal benefits, even when a member of their household is eligible to receive them. They are also less likely to participate in assistance programs for which undocumented immigrants qualify, such as the Special Supplemental Nutrition Program for Women, Infants, and Children (WIC). This program provides food vouchers for low-income pregnant women, nursing mothers, and children under five years old, as well as breastfeeding support and nutrition education. Nearly 8 million people—three-quarters of them children—participate in the program, with the average participant receiving about forty-five dollars in vouchers each month.

> "Our projections suggest that the presence of unauthorized workers in the United States has, on average, a positive effect on the financial status of the Social Security program."[15]
>
> —Social Security Administration

Soon after Trump's inauguration in early 2017, WIC officials noticed that many undocumented immigrants were dropping out of the program. "We've heard a lot of stories about people who either wouldn't show up for appointments, or who wanted to withdraw from the program, cancel their benefits and be scrubbed from the record,"[16] says Douglas Greenaway, the president and chief executive officer of the National WIC Association.

Fear and confusion about future Trump administration immigration policies likely fueled the undocumented immigrants' desire to stay out of sight.

Some anti-immigrant groups believe that the modest WIC benefit provided to some undocumented immigrants presents a strain on public services. However, most data indicates that reducing WIC benefits could actually increase the national cost of health care for all Americans. Studies have consistently found that participation in WIC by low-income families leads to healthier children. Participating children are more likely to receive immunizations and less likely to suffer from malnutrition, obesity, or related conditions such as diabetes. Healthy children and families cost the public less than unhealthy children and families. According to a study of child poverty conducted by the American Academy of Pediatrics, that difference in health care costs could be as much as $22 billion to $26 billion a year.

More Access to Services Would Benefit Taxpayers

Ironically, allowing undocumented immigrants to access other public assistance programs might actually reduce, rather than increase, the amount of public services they use. For example, an estimated 3.9 million undocumented immigrants do not have health insurance. They must seek treatment for routine care and medical emergencies in hospital emergency rooms. Many hospitals receive federal funding and by law are not permitted to turn people away even if they cannot pay for their care. Emergency care is extremely expensive compared to conventional medical treatment, particularly with regard to health conditions that could be prevented or managed through proper attention, such as diabetes or heart disease.

If undocumented immigrants were permitted to purchase inexpensive family health care plans under a government-managed program like the Affordable Care Act, they would no longer have to rely on hospitals for care. This would reduce the overall cost of health care and result in savings to American taxpayers. But even without such a change, it is clear that what undocumented immigrants contribute to the US economy and to state and local governments through their taxes is more valuable than the public services that they do use.

Illegal Immigration Strains Public Services

"It is silly to deny that the influx of nearly 11 million illegal immigrants—mostly low-skilled adults and their children—strain resources in public schools and for other social services. And this most harshly affects the quality and availability of education and assistance to the poorest Americans."

—Peter Morici, economist and professor of business at the University of Maryland

Peter Morici, "The Real Cost of Illegal Immigration," *Washington (DC) Times*, September 6, 2016. www.washingtontimes.com.

Consider these questions as you read:

1. Do you believe the children of undocumented immigrants should be allowed to attend public schools in the United States? Why or why not?
2. Is it fair that hospital emergency rooms are required to treat everyone, regardless of their immigration status or ability to pay? Why or why not?
3. Taking into account the facts and ideas presented in this discussion, how persuasive is the argument that illegal immigration unfairly strains public services? Which arguments are strongest and why?

Editor's note: The discussion that follows presents common arguments made in support of this perspective, reinforced by facts, quotes, and examples taken from various sources.

Illegal immigrants may not be eligible for the major social insurance or welfare programs, but they still receive many government-provided—and thus taxpayer-funded—services. Illegal immigrant families receive public education for their children, and school districts often must spend additional money on teachers and programs to accommodate non-English-speaking students. The American health care system is structured in such a way that hospitals must provide medical treatment to illegal immigrants even if they cannot pay for it. Illegal immigrant families with US-born children often receive aid through federal and state government welfare programs, because their children are citizens who are eligible for these programs. Finally, illegal immigrants use the roads, parks, water and sewerage systems, police, and fire protection in the communities where they live. As the illegal population grows, local and state governments often must construct new infrastructure or hire additional people to accommodate this larger number of people.

American taxpayers wind up paying these costs. Federal agencies estimate that about half of all illegal immigrants work off the books, taking jobs in which they are paid in cash. Because these payments are not reported to the government, they are not taxed. The other half of the illegal immigrant workforce does have payroll taxes deducted from paychecks, some of which goes to fund government social welfare and health programs like Medicare and Social Security. However, low-income illegal immigrants who file tax returns generally receive some of their taxes back in the form of tax credits. So the taxes that illegal immigrants pay into the system are tens of billions of dollars less than the cost of the government services they use.

A Burden on School Districts

In 2015, according to the most recent data from the US Census Bureau, between 2.9 million and 3.8 million children of illegal immigrants were enrolled in American public schools. These children often present several challenges for school districts. One is that children from non-English-speaking countries often require costly English as a Second Language (ESL) programs. These programs can be expensive to implement, since the districts must often hire additional teachers and provide classroom space in school buildings that are already crowded. Compounding this challenge is the fact that many illegal immigrants are not well educated themselves, so their children are often less prepared to enter the educational system than other children are.

Although federal laws require public schools to provide ESL programs when they are needed, a relatively small share of school funding comes from the federal government. On average, federal funds make up less than 5 percent of the total budgets for most public schools. In many states, school districts are funded predominantly through property taxes, which are derived from the value of properties in the community and are assessed by local or state governments. This means that local taxpayers pay the bulk of the cost for their school districts.

Neighborhoods with large numbers of illegal immigrants tend to have lower property values than other communities. The school districts that serve these neighborhoods generally struggle to raise the funds needed to provide a good education. Because school taxes are assessed as a percentage of property value, low-income communities cannot raise as much money to pay for quality educational programs. Statistics from the US Department of Education indicate that each year, high-income districts raise over 15 percent more in taxes for education than low-income districts do. The need for expensive ESL programs in school districts that are already strapped for cash presents an unfair burden to poorer Americans who live in those districts.

A Burden on the Health Care System

Like the public school system, the American health care system is also stretched thin as it attempts to serve illegal immigrants. By law, all hospitals that receive federal Medicare or Medicaid funds must evaluate the medical condition of all individuals who present themselves at the emergency room. If a person is found to have a medical condition—including being in labor with a baby—the hospital is required to treat the patient, regardless of his or her ability to pay for that treatment.

Many illegal immigrants fall into this category. The Kaiser Family Foundation estimates that there are about 3.9 million illegal immigrants who do not have health insurance. Often, these people use emergency rooms as their primary health care option, even for minor conditions. This places several stresses on the health care system. Overuse of emergency rooms by illegal immigrants results in overcrowding, which affects

Taxpayers Spend Billions on Illegal Immigrants

Illegal immigration places a significant strain on taxpayers and the services they fund through their tax dollars. This is the conclusion of a 2017 report by the Federation for American Immigration Reform (FAIR). FAIR found that US taxpayers contribute approximately $135 billion in federal, state, and local taxes to cover health, education, social service, and other costs incurred by illegal immigrants and their families. Even when that amount is offset by the tax contributions of illegal immigrants ($19 billion), the taxpayer burden ($116 billion)—and strain on public services—is huge.

The Fiscal Burden of Illegal Immigration on US Taxpayers

Total Expenditures (on Illegal Immigrants)	
Total Federal Expenditures	$46 billion
Total State and Local Expenditures	+ $89 billion
Total National Expenditures	**$135 billion**
Total Tax Contributions (by Illegal Immigrants)	
Total Federal Taxes Paid	$15 billion
Plus Total State and Local Taxes Paid	+ $4 billion
Total Tax Contributions	**$19 billion**
Total Cost of Illegal Immigration	
Total National Expenditures	$135 billion
Minus Total Tax Contributions	− $19 billion
Total Fiscal Cost of Illegal Immigrants on Taxpayers	**$116 billion**

Source: Matthew O'Brien et al., "The Fiscal Burden of Illegal Immigration on United States Taxpayers (2017)," Federation for American Immigration Reform, September 27, 2017. www.fairus.org.

the care that hospitals provide to other patients. And hospitals must cover the expense of uncompensated emergency room treatment by charging their other patients higher fees.

Another way that illegal immigrants receive vital health services is through Emergency Medicaid, a federal program that ensures they will be treated for acute medical situations that result in severe pain and place a patient's health in jeopardy. The services covered can vary by state: New York and New Jersey cover the cost of chemotherapy and other cancer treatments, for example, while Arizona and Georgia do not. Most of those participating in the Emergency Medicaid program are illegal immigrants. The program costs federal taxpayers more than $2 billion per year. An additional cost is borne by taxpayers in states like New York and New Jersey, which cover services that are not included in the federal program guidelines.

The government provides limited health care to illegal immigrants through a network of roughly twelve hundred community health centers located throughout the country. These centers, which are funded with federal tax dollars, provide basic medical treatment, dental care, and mental health services to everyone, regardless of immigration status or ability to pay. In addition, a number of states have expanded their Medicaid programs so that they provide health care to all children, regardless of their immigration status. California, Illinois, Massachusetts, New York, and Washington use state rather than federal funding to pay the cost of medical treatment for illegal immigrant children. (The District of Columbia has a similar arrangement.)

> "The total cost of illegal immigration to U.S. taxpayers is both staggering and crippling."[17]
>
> — Federation for American Immigration Reform

Overall, experts estimate that American taxpayers spend about $18.5 billion a year to cover the health care expenses of uninsured illegal immigrants. That figure includes about $11.2 billion paid by federal taxes—even though the current policy of the federal government is to prohibit unauthorized immigrants from accessing federal health care programs such as Medicaid or government-run health care exchanges.

A High Cost to US Taxpayers

Education and health care are two major areas in which illegal immigrants receive far more in benefits than they pay in taxes and service fees.

But federal, state, and local governments incur many other expenses to support illegal immigrant populations. A 2017 study by the Federation for American Immigration Reform (FAIR) estimated that the cost to society of illegal immigrants and their US-born children exceeds $134 billion a year. FAIR found that the federal government spends about $48 billion annually on services for illegal immigrants, while state and local governments combined spend roughly $89 billion.

Subtracting the annual tax contributions of illegal immigrants—about $15.4 billion in federal taxes and another $3.5 billion in state and local taxes—helps reduce the total cost. However, the FAIR study concluded that the difference between the cost of government-provided services and the amount illegal immigrants pay in taxes is nearly $116 billion a year. "The total cost of illegal immigration to U.S. taxpayers is both staggering and crippling," note the FAIR study's authors. "In 2013, FAIR estimated the total cost to be approximately $113 billion. So, in under four years, the cost has risen nearly $3 billion. This is a disturbing and unsustainable trend."[17]

This result of FAIR's analysis matches earlier studies, conducted by the conservative Heritage Foundation and by the nonpartisan Government Accountability Office. Both concluded that illegal immigrants generate more in costs than revenues to federal, state, and local governments. Therefore, the presence of illegal immigrants in the United States places an unfair burden on the American citizens and legal immigrants whose taxes support public education, the health care system, and other government programs.

Chapter Three

Are Stronger Border Enforcement Measures Needed?

Stronger Border Enforcement Measures Are Needed

- A real wall, not just a hodgepodge of fences and barriers here and there, is essential.
- Even a real wall will not get the job done; more agents are needed for border enforcement.
- For the agents to be truly effective, they need improved technology.

The Debate at a Glance

Stronger Border Enforcement Measures Are Not Needed

- Current border enforcement measures are already working.
- New border walls and stricter enforcement at the borders will not have much effect since most illegal immigrants are visa overstayers.
- The United States should try to fix the problem at its source rather than throw money at simplistic measures like walls.

Stronger Border Enforcement Measures Are Needed

"Every place they have built a wall or a barrier it has worked. One hundred percent of the time illegal migration has decreased wherever there's a barrier put."

—Tom Homan, former acting director of US Immigration and Customs Enforcement

Quoted in Ari Shapiro, "Director of ICE Discusses Immigration Enforcement and Proposals," *All Things Considered*, NPR, January 26, 2018. www.npr.org.

Consider these questions as you read:

1. In your opinion, is it a problem that people are able to cross the US border illegally? Why or why not?
2. Do you believe that physical barriers are the best way to keep undocumented immigrants from entering the United States? Why or why not?
3. If it were your decision, how would you control the nation's borders?

Editor's note: The discussion that follows presents common arguments made in support of this perspective, reinforced by facts, quotes, and examples taken from various sources.

Every day, several thousand people from Mexico or Central America try to cross the roughly 2,000-mile-long (3,219 km) border between the United States and Mexico, hoping to find work in the United States. Over the past fifteen years, the US government has enacted numerous measures to prevent illegal border crossings. In 2006 Congress authorized the construction of roughly 600 miles (957 km) of walls and barriers in parts of Arizona, California, New Mexico, and Texas. The border walls have worked, enabling US Border Patrol officers to intercept many illegal crossers before they could disappear into populated areas.

These walls and other security measures have helped slow the flood of illegal immigrants. But there are still too many people who cross our porous border illegally each year. In a 2016 report, the US Department of Homeland Security estimated that Border Patrol catches about 54 percent of those who try to cross the border illegally. If that figure is correct, then 300,000 to 350,000 foreigners are making it into the United States illegally but successfully each year.

Part of the problem is that the existing border fences are just not adequate. About half of the current fencing consists of steel vehicle barriers, 4 to 6 feet (1.2 to 1.8 m) high, which were designed to prevent vehicles from crossing the border. However, migrants who are on foot can easily climb over them or even walk through spaces between the steel posts. Even the existing "pedestrian fences" can be climbed by determined immigrants with ladders or ropes, and there are numerous gaps in the walls. Tunnels under the walls have also been discovered.

To reduce illegal border crossings, the United States will need to take a multifaceted security approach. First, the existing walls should be expanded and improved so that they actually prevent people from crossing the border. In the past, however, immigrants have proved to be creative; some will find ways around even the highest walls. So, more Border Patrol agents are needed. Finally, the efforts of those agents must be supplemented by investing in new, more effective technology.

Build a Wall

Donald Trump has proposed building a new wall that would protect more of the border. He has also called for improvements in sections of wall that currently exist in high-traffic areas. Trump's proposal has been criticized as being expensive and unnecessary. But Border Patrol and Homeland Security officials—the people responsible for preventing undocumented aliens from entering the United States—overwhelmingly agree that border walls are among the most effective methods of preventing illegal entry into the United States. "We are committed to keeping America safe by securing our borders, and that includes enhancing our border wall system," explained Carla Provost, the acting chief of the

Many Americans Support Stronger Border Security Measures

Many Americans (61 percent) think border security is inadequate, and just over half (54 percent) want to see a combination of physical and electronic barriers erected along the US-Mexico border. This is the finding of a January 2018 Harvard-Harris Poll. The Harvard-Harris Poll is a collaboration between Harvard University's Center for American Political Studies and the Harris Poll organization.

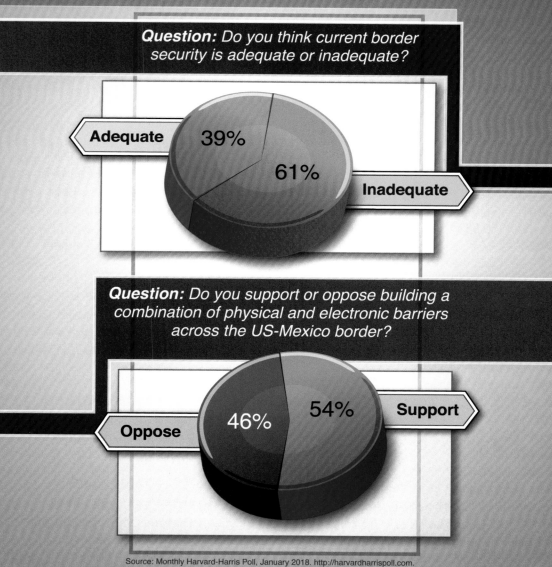

Question: Do you think current border security is adequate or inadequate?

Adequate 39%

61% Inadequate

Question: Do you support or oppose building a combination of physical and electronic barriers across the US-Mexico border?

Oppose 46%

54% Support

Source: Monthly Harvard-Harris Poll, January 2018. http://harvardharrispoll.com.

Border Patrol, in March 2018. "In our experience, walls work. With the right combination of a wall, technology, infrastructure, and agents, we have been successful in denying and impeding illegal border crossers."[18]

A few days after his inauguration in January 2017, Trump directed US Customs and Border Protection to build and test prototypes for the new wall. In March 2018 eight prototypes were shown to the public. These walls, made out of concrete or steel, were 18 to 30 feet (5.5 to 9 m) high, as well as 6 feet (1.8 m) below ground to deter tunnelers. The walls have been tested by military teams to see which of the prototypes can best prevent breaching, climbing, or digging, but a decision had not been made as of the fall of 2018. As the wall proposal is fully developed, it is incumbent upon Congress to provide the funding and authorization needed to construct the new wall.

Hire More Border Patrol Officers

Building a higher and stronger wall that covers more of the southern border is only one element of the solution. Walls can slow migrants' progress, but even the highest wall will not stop a truly determined migrant from crossing. Those who find ways over, under, or through the wall will eventually be able to find a safe place on the US side of the border unless a robust force of Border Patrol agents is able to quickly intercept them once they cross.

> "We are committed to keeping America safe by securing our borders, and that includes enhancing our border wall system."[18]
>
> —Carla Provost, acting chief of the US Border Patrol

In January 2017 Trump signed an executive order calling for the Border Patrol to hire five thousand additional officers. Unfortunately, inaction in Congress has thwarted this essential element of border security. During budget negotiations in 2017 and 2018, Congress refused to allocate funds for the additional Border Patrol officers.

More officers are desperately needed. In 2013 the Border Patrol had more than 18,600 officers working along the southwestern border. Since then, that number has been declining steadily. Today there are about

16,600 Border Patrol officers working in that sector. Border Patrol agents are leaving faster than they can be replaced because other law enforcement jobs are much more appealing. In 2017, 39 percent of officers who left the Border Patrol went to work for other federal agencies that paid better. US Customs and Border Protection also has strict vetting policies for new hires, including extensive polygraph tests, which two out of three applicants fail.

Again, gridlock in Congress has contributed to the problem. Since Trump's election, several measures have been introduced that would make it easier to recruit and retain Border Patrol agents by easing the vetting process and increasing the pay. However, these measures have stalled thus far. They must be considered immediately to help expand the Border Patrol to its proper size. As the late Arizona senator John McCain commented about one piece of legislation in 2017, "We can't effectively secure our southern border if we don't have the manpower to get the job done."[19]

> "We can't effectively secure our southern border if we don't have the manpower to get the job done."[19]
>
> —Arizona senator John McCain

Use Better Surveillance Technology

To help Border Patrol officers effectively control the nation's borders, the implementation and use of new technology is crucial. At present, agents are forced to use outdated technology. Motion-activated video cameras were once considered state of the art for border surveillance, but not anymore. Nelson Balido, a former member of the Homeland Security Advisory Council, explains:

> Thousands of man hours are effectively wasted every week as blurry-eyed agents or contractors sift through images seeking anything suspicious. They certainly get their share of bunny rabbits and skunks, because some of those cameras cannot tell the difference—they just detect movement. . . . 99.9 percent of suspicious activity picked up by cameras turns out to be false alarms.[20]

Similarly, says Balido, the network of motion-detecting ground sensors deployed in many areas is outdated when compared to current technology. Ground sensors can alert agents that something has moved across the border, but it cannot tell them what it is. The disturbance is just as likely to be caused by a deer or a goat as a group of illegal border crossers. Maintenance of the sensors is also labor intensive. "There are agents whose sole, unenviable job is to go around replacing the sensors' batteries,"[21] Balido notes.

New technology exists and should be made available to border agents. Light detection and ranging (LIDAR) technology, for instance, would use lasers to create a three-dimensional digital map of the border area. When the LIDAR system detects a disturbance, a computer would analyze the movement to determine whether it is small animal, which could be ignored, or an unauthorized human trying to cross the border. A human border crosser would immediately trigger an alert, allowing agents to respond quickly and in the correct location. The LIDAR system would also show agents where a border crosser is headed. Such a system could be implemented in areas where walls would be difficult or prohibitively expensive to construct due to the terrain.

Upgrading the use of technology on the border is going to be expensive, and so is building a better wall and increasing the number of Border Patrol agents. But the price of doing nothing to secure America's borders will undoubtedly be even higher, as the growing illegal immigrant population burdens public resources like hospitals, schools, police, and firefighters. The federal government needs to fund these commonsense measures to gain control of the border and prevent illegal immigrants from continuing to exploit our system.

Stronger Border Enforcement Measures Are Not Needed

"I know from personal and professional experience that a physical wall would be ineffective at reducing the number of undocumented people and the amount of illegal drugs that come across the border into the United States. . . . We can't double down on a 14th century solution to a 21st century challenge if we want a viable long-term solution."

—US Representative Henry Cuellar of Texas

Henry Cuellar, "The Answer to Border Security Is Technology, Not a Wall," CNN, January 11, 2018. www.cnn.com.

Consider these questions as you read:

1. How convincing is the argument that a wall is not needed? Explain your answer.
2. What are some of the reasons given for why fewer migrants are getting caught trying to cross the border? What might be some additional reasons?
3. Do you think it is a valid use of taxpayer funds for the United States to provide financial aid that is used to improve the standard of living in other countries? Why or why not?

Editor's note: The discussion that follows presents common arguments made in support of this perspective, reinforced by facts, quotes, and examples taken from various sources.

"Our Southern Border is under siege,"[22] declared Donald Trump in May 2018, reiterating his past demands to construct a wall along the border between the United States and Mexico. Trump has consistently characterized the 2,000-mile-long (3,219 km) US-Mexico border as being easy for foreigners to cross. However, two decades' worth of data provided by the federal government refutes such statements. According to US Customs and Border Protection, the number of people who have tried to sneak across the border has declined sharply since 2000. That year, Border Patrol agents caught over 1.6 million undocumented immigrants attempting to cross the US-Mexico border. Since then, the annual number of apprehensions has steadily declined, falling to around three hundred thousand a year by 2017.

The steep reduction in illegal border crossing attempts can be credited to a variety of government policies that have been implemented since the late 1990s. Since that time the United States has spent more than $7 billion to construct and maintain more than 600 miles (957 km) of barriers in the border areas where most illegal crossings took place. The number of agents assigned to protect US borders has also risen during this time, from fewer than five thousand agents in 1995 to nearly twenty thousand agents in 2018. The Department of Homeland Security also invested more than $1.1 billion in a program called the Secure Border Initiative to use technology such as mobile radars, motion sensors, and unmanned aerial drones in certain hard-to-patrol areas.

Clearly, the current policies in place to defend the borders are working. Even Trump can admit this, albeit grudgingly. "We have a lousy wall over here now but at least it stops 90, 95 percent,"[23] Trump acknowledged in March 2018. Since current programs are effective, there is no need to spend billions more to build a border wall or increase border enforcement efforts.

The Wall Would Be Highly Expensive

Trump's obsession with preventing illegal immigrants from crossing the southern border became more public during his 2016 presidential campaign. During an August 2016 campaign stop in Phoenix, Arizona, Trump proclaimed, "On Day One, we will begin working on an impenetrable, physical, tall, powerful, beautiful southern border wall."[24] As president, Trump has continued to push for this prohibitively expensive project.

During his presidential campaign, Trump estimated that it would cost around $8 billion to $12 billion to construct the wall. However, the actual cost is likely to be much higher. In 2018 the Trump administration asked Congress for $18 billion for the border wall project. That amount would only pay for about 300 miles (483 km) of barriers—some of which would upgrade existing fences, not cover new areas.

Consequently, most independent experts agree that the actual cost of building Trump's wall would be considerably higher than the president has proposed. It could be $40 billion or more, due to the difficulty of construction along the border. "President Trump's wall would be a mammoth expenditure that would have little impact on illegal immigration," notes David Bier, a policy analyst at the Cato Institute. "[The wall] will harm the lives of thousands of border residents and immigrants while wasting billions of tax dollars."[25]

> "President Trump's wall would be a mammoth expenditure that would have little impact on illegal immigration."[25]
>
> —David Bier, Cato Institute policy analyst

What is more, a solid majority of American taxpayers are not interested in paying for this wall. Opinion polls conducted between 2015 and 2018 have consistently found that about 60 percent of respondents oppose massive spending on a border wall. "The American people have little interest in a wall and rate it one of the least important things the president could do at this point,"[26] Gallup Poll editor in chief Frank Newport observes in a review of opinion poll data drawn from multiple sources.

Leaky Borders Are Not the Problem

Trump's proposals to increase border security do not take into account the reality of undocumented immigration in the United States today. Most undocumented immigrants did not wade across the Rio Grande or scale fences along the border. Instead, most entered the United States with legal visas, either for work or tourism, and did not leave the country when their visas expired. A 2017 analysis of US Department of Homeland Security data, published in the *Journal on Migration and Human*

Illegal Border Crossing Arrests Have Fallen

Current border security policies have sharply reduced the number of illegal border crossing attempts over the past two decades. The 310,531 arrests on the border reported by US Customs and Border Protection in fiscal year 2017 represents the lowest figure since the early 1970s. Stronger border enforcement measures are unnecessary; they would be a waste of money and resources.

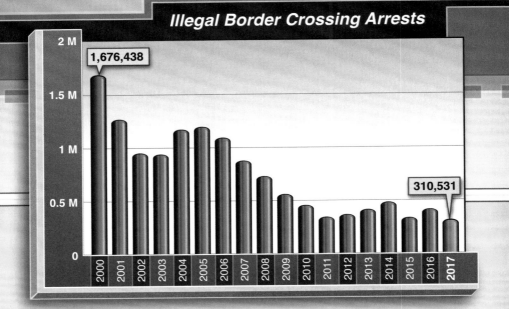

Illegal Border Crossing Arrests

Source: John Burnett, "Arrests for Illegal Border Crossings Hit 46-Year Low," National Public Radio, December 5, 2017.www.npr.org.

Security, found that from 2007 to 2014, roughly two-thirds of undocumented immigrants had overstayed their visas.

The Homeland Security data indicates that many of the undocumented immigrants who have crossed the border since 2005 came from the so-called Northern Triangle states of Central America: El Salvador, Guatemala, and Honduras. These three countries are among the most violent places in the world, and more than 100,000 migrants flee from them each year, hoping to escape the violence and poverty. Those refugees often request political asylum at the US border due to the dangerous conditions in their home countries. Most are coming because they fear for their lives. Clearly, spending billions on a border wall and stricter enforcement will not slow this stream of desperate migrants. Robert Warren and Donald Kerwin, authors of the Homeland Security study, conclude:

> The striking change in the mode of arrival after 2005 raises important policy questions not just about the need for a 2,000-mile wall, but about the allocation of immigration enforcement resources and funding levels for border enforcement compared to other strategies that might reduce new arrivals into the undocumented population and strategies to reduce the overall size of this population. . . . Shifts in the allocation of resources would address the primary source of undocumented immigration—overstaying temporary visas—and the causes of the flight of large numbers of migrants from the violence-plagued [Central American] states to the United States and elsewhere.[27]

Address Root Causes Instead

As long as the United States provides more work opportunities and safer conditions than neighboring countries, there will be people who try to enter the country illegally. However, rather than investing billions of dollars to build walls and develop more stringent border enforcement measures, the United States would be better served addressing the problems that drive migrants here from neighboring states.

One option would be to work with Central American governments by funding programs that would enable them to reduce violence and poverty by building the infrastructure needed to develop strong, job-producing economies. In 2014 the United States encouraged the governments of El Salvador, Guatemala, and Honduras to develop an initiative called the Alliance for Prosperity. The purpose of this program is to develop economic opportunities, improve public safety, enhance access to the legal system, and strengthen institutions in those Central American states. Funding for projects such as hydroelectric dams, better roads, and improvements to ports comes from the Northern Triangle states and investment from private companies. If the US government were to commit $1 billion a year to the Alliance for Prosperity, it would be far less expensive—and far more effective—than building Trump's wall.

This is the view of Jason Marczak of the Atlantic Council, an international affairs think tank that supports programs like the Alliance for Prosperity. Marczak explains:

> The key to preventing unauthorized migration from Central America is to improve the conditions in the countries themselves. . . . Unless the impetus to leave the country changes it doesn't matter how strong a border the United States has when people are without hope, opportunity, worried about survival, fleeing violence—domestic as well as gang violence. Conditions can be so bad in certain communities of the Northern Triangle that it doesn't matter how tough the journey north is, if you're living a life of such despair you are going to migrate.[28]

Spending billions of dollars to achieve a marginal, incremental improvement in the number of undocumented immigrants stopped at the border does not make sense. As Mark L. Schneider, an advisor for the International Crisis Group, notes, "The only lasting answer to illegal migration is to address the conditions of poverty, violence and criminal impunity that force families to flee their homes in Central America."[29]

Chapter Four

Should Illegal Immigrants Be Given a Path to Citizenship?

Illegal Immigrants Should Be Given a Path to Citizenship

- Polls show broad support for allowing undocumented immigrants to eventually become US citizens.
- Studies show that legal status and a path to citizenship would bring about significant economic growth.
- The alternative to a path to citizenship is mass deportation, which would be costly and violate cherished American principles.

The Debate at a Glance

Illegal Immigrants Should Not Be Given a Path to Citizenship

- Allowing people who are living in the United States illegally to become US citizens would be unfair to all those immigrants who followed the rules.
- A path to legal status but not full citizenship might be appropriate in some cases.
- Experience has shown that few illegal immigrants will take advantage of a path to citizenship, because they intend to eventually return to their home countries.

Illegal Immigrants Should Be Given a Path to Citizenship

"These young people have lived in America since they were children and built their lives here. There is support across the country for allowing Dreamers—who have records of achievement—to stay, work, and reach their full potential. We should not squander these young people's talents and penalize our own nation."

—US senator Lindsey Graham, cosponsor of the 2017 DREAM Act

Quoted in Lindsay Graham: US Senator, South Carolina, "Graham, Durbin Introduce Bipartisan Dream Act to Give Immigrant Students a Path to Citizenship," press release, July 20, 2017. www.lgraham.senate.gov.

Consider these questions as you read:

1. Do you believe that young people brought to the United States illegally by their parents should be able to become citizens? Why or why not?
2. Do you believe that all undocumented immigrants, regardless of age, should have an opportunity to gain US citizenship? Why or why not?
3. How would you view mass deportation of undocumented immigrants?

Editor's note: The discussion that follows presents common arguments made in support of this perspective, reinforced by facts, quotes, and examples taken from various sources.

Since 2012 more than 700,000 undocumented immigrants have enrolled in a program called Deferred Action for Childhood Arrivals, or DACA. This program, enacted by Barack Obama, was intended to delay the deportation of young people who were brought into the United States illegally as children. Those eligible for DACA were brought by their parents before they were sixteen years old. Some may not have even realized they were living in the country illegally until they were older and found themselves without the documentation they needed to get a good job, apply to college, join the military, or get a driver's license.

To participate in DACA, immigrants were required to pay a $495 fee and register with the government. In exchange, they received permission to live and work or study in the country for two years. This status, which could be renewed, did not grant all of the same rights held by legal immigrants. It did allow this group of young undocumented immigrants to pursue higher education, get driver's licenses, and receive health insurance from their employers or through state-funded programs.

In September 2017 the Trump administration announced that it would stop accepting applicants to DACA immediately and that in six months the two-year protective terms would no longer be renewable. Trump's decision means that hundreds of thousands of young people are vulnerable to deportation—a frightening prospect, since many have no memory of any home other than the United States.

For now, lawsuits have protected those already enrolled in DACA from being removed from the country. However, their future, along with that of millions of others who are living illegally in the country, remains uncertain.

Americans Support a Path to Citizenship

Public opinion polls taken over the past few years consistently show that most Americans support a path to citizenship for undocumented immigrants who were brought to the United States as children. In a June 2018 Gallup Poll, 83 percent of respondents favored a proposal to allow "immigrants, who were brought to the U.S. illegally as children, the chance to become U.S. citizens if they meet certain requirements over a period of time."[30] A CBS News poll taken around the same time found that 87 percent of respondents favored allowing the young immigrants to remain, so long as they were working, going to school, or serving in the military.

An amnesty program that would provide a path to US citizenship would affect at least 1.8 million people—the estimated number of undocumented immigrants eligible for DACA. Expanding such a program to include those who were under age eighteen when they were brought to the United States would double the number of eligible immigrants to about 3.6 million. The media often calls this population "Dreamers," since they would have been eligible for citizenship under the Development, Relief, and Education for Alien Minors (DREAM) Act—legislation introduced in Congress in 2001 that was never passed.

Even Trump has said that he is open to an immigration plan that would provide a pathway to citizenship for the Dreamers. "It's going to happen, at some point in the future, over a period of 10 to 12 years,"[31] Trump predicted in January 2018.

While young Dreamers have gotten most of the attention in the media, opinion polls indicate that many Americans support a path to citizenship for all undocumented immigrants, regardless of age. According to a Fox News September 2017 poll, 83 percent of respondents "support setting up a system for all illegal immigrants who are currently working in the country to become legal residents."[32] Conferring legal status on these immigrants would enable them to begin the process of applying for full US citizenship. Support for this idea has steadily grown among Americans over the past few years. In 2016, 74 percent of respondents supported a path to legal residency (and eventual citizenship) for all undocumented immigrants, up from 64 percent in 2015.

> "[Eighty-three percent of respondents] support setting up a system for all illegal immigrants who are currently working in the country to become legal residents."[32]
>
> —Fox News poll

Amnesty Provides Economic Benefits

A reason for this growing support may be that Americans recognize that immigrant workers help the economy. Studies have indicated that legal status and a path to citizenship could bring about significant economic growth. For example, a 2017 study by the Center for American Progress found that allowing the Dreamers to earn legal status (and eventually

Most Americans Support a Path to Citizenship

In a June 2018 poll by the Gallup Organization, 83 percent of Americans said they strongly favored or favored a proposal to allow immigrants who were brought to the United States illegally as children the chance to become citizens if they meet certain criteria. Only 15 percent of respondents expressed some level of opposition to such a proposal.

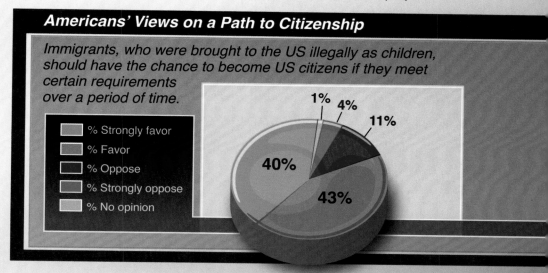

Americans' Views on a Path to Citizenship

Immigrants, who were brought to the US illegally as children, should have the chance to become US citizens if they meet certain requirements over a period of time.

- % Strongly favor
- % Favor
- % Oppose
- % Strongly oppose
- % No opinion

1% 4% 11% 40% 43%

Source: Frank Newport, "Americans Oppose Border Walls, Favor Dealing with DACA," Gallup Organization, June 20, 2018. https://news.gallup.com.

citizenship) could increase the US gross domestic product (GDP) by $400 billion to $1 trillion over a ten-year period. "Overall, the data from this study are clear," write the study's authors. "Passing the Dream Act would significantly improve the American economy."[33]

These figures are aligned with an earlier study conducted by the Center for American Progress that projected how amnesty for all undocumented immigrants would affect the economy. In that scenario, GDP would grow by $1.4 trillion over a ten-year period, and the US economy would create, on average, an additional 203,000 jobs per year. "Legal status and a road map to citizenship for the unauthorized will bring about significant economic gains in terms of growth, earnings, tax revenues,

> "Legal status and a road map to citizenship for the unauthorized will bring about significant economic gains in terms of growth, earnings, tax revenues, and jobs."[34]
>
> —Robert Lynch and Patrick Oakford, Center for American Progress

and jobs—all of which will not occur in the absence of immigration reform or with reform that creates a permanent sub-citizen class of residents,"[34] conclude study authors Robert Lynch and Patrick Oakford.

Both of these results are in line with projections made by the Congressional Budget Office, a nonpartisan federal agency that analyzes legislation being considered by Congress. In 2014 the agency estimated that passage of the DREAM Act would increase US GDP by $700 billion over the first decade. In addition, during that ten-year period, newly legal immigrants would pay over $800 billion in taxes, including approximately $300 billion in Social Security taxes. That represents a huge benefit to all Americans.

Mass Deportation Would Be Expensive and Immoral

At present, however, citizenship for the nation's undocumented population is not possible. Existing laws require undocumented immigrants to be caught and deported. For decades, law enforcement has prioritized the deportation of illegal immigrants who have broken laws or are involved in gang activity. Undocumented immigrants who have stayed out of trouble have largely been ignored. That is changing. The government has increased its deportation efforts. However, there is no realistic way for mass deportations to occur without a huge investment in law enforcement and surveillance technology.

Whereas a path to citizenship would help the US economy grow, studies show that mass deportations would have the opposite effect. One recent study published by the American Action Forum found that a program of mass deportations would cost the government approximately $419 billion to $619 billion over a twenty-year period. This would also reduce the US labor force by 8 million workers, which would cause the economy to contract. "As a result, 20 years from now the economy would be nearly 6 percent or $1.6 trillion smaller than it would be if the government did not remove all undocumented immigrants," write study authors Ben Gitis and Laura Collins. "While this impact would be found throughout the economy, the agriculture, construction, retail and hospitality sectors would be especially strongly affected."[35]

Mass deportation would turn the United States into a police state, and families that have lived here for years would be torn apart. "Most of these immigrants have been here a long time," noted Obama in a 2014 speech. "They work hard, often in tough, low-paying jobs. They support their families. They worship at our churches. . . . Their hopes, dreams, and patriotism are just like ours. As my predecessor, President Bush, once put it: 'They are a part of American life.'"[36]

It would certainly be fair for the undocumented to have to wait a little longer and work a little harder under any path to citizenship. They should not be permitted to "cut in line" ahead of immigrants who followed the rules and came here legally. But undocumented immigrants who have stayed out of trouble, worked hard, and paid taxes should have the opportunity to eventually become citizens. After all, that is the foundation of the American dream: that anyone can succeed if he or she is willing to work hard and accept the responsibilities of citizenship.

Illegal Immigrants Should Not Be Given a Path to Citizenship

"Fairness and equality under the law are fundamental American principles. Amnesty proposals, however, reward those who have broken the law. Beyond incentivizing additional illegal immigration, amnesty is unfair to all law-abiding Americans, legal immigrants, and those waiting to come legally to the U.S. . . . Ultimately, amnesty unfairly favors those who have broken U.S. laws at the expense of those who obey them."

—David Inserra, immigration policy analyst at the Heritage Foundation

David Inserra, "Dreaming of Amnesty: Legalization Will Spur More Illegal Immigration," Heritage Foundation, October 30, 2017. www.heritage.org.

Consider these questions as you read:

1. Do you believe that measures to reduce illegal immigration (such as tighter border security, stronger controls on visa overstays, and hiring restrictions) should be implemented before amnesty is offered? Why or why not?
2. How persuasive is the argument that illegal immigrants will leave the country on their own if prevented from working? Why?
3. If you were living here illegally and given the opportunity to remain in the United States legally but without the possibility of obtaining citizenship, would you do that? Why or why not?

Editor's note: The discussion that follows presents common arguments made in support of this perspective, reinforced by facts, quotes, and examples taken from various sources.

A citizen is a legal inhabitant of a country who is granted certain rights or privileges that noncitizens do not have. In the United States, citizens have an opportunity to participate in national life by voting in elections, serving on juries, or running for government office. Under the Constitution, any person born in the United States automatically becomes a US citizen. Immigrants, however, cannot automatically become citizens. Those who have gone through all the steps to receive a green card—legal authorization to live and work in the United States—can eventually become US citizens through a process called naturalization. This process often takes five years or more to complete and ends with a ceremony in which the immigrant promises to support and defend the Constitution and the laws of the United States, pay taxes, and serve the nation when required.

One reason immigrants seek US citizenship is that it is much easier for naturalized citizens to permanently move foreign-born family members to the United States. Naturalized US citizens can file an immigrant visa petition on behalf of a spouse, a parent, or an unmarried child under age eighteen. These visas will be automatically granted. Citizens can also file visa petitions for older children and siblings, although these must go through the normal review process. Immigrants with a green card can only apply for an immigrant visa for their spouse or unmarried child, and their visas requests can be denied.

US citizenship is extremely valuable. It should not be conferred on people who have entered the United States without permission or who knowingly violated the law by overstaying their visa. Illegal immigrants should not receive any benefit as a result of their illegal activity—and definitely not US citizenship. To offer this coveted status would be unfair to all those immigrants who followed the rules, lived and worked in the country legally, and persevered through the naturalization process.

Amnesty Encourages Others to Break the Rules

In recent years, lawmakers in Congress have proposed a number of bills that, if enacted into law, would provide amnesty for certain illegal immigrants. Some of them, such as the DREAM Act and the Recognizing America's Children Act, include provisions that would enable illegal

Amnesty Encourages More Illegal Border Crossers

An amnesty program that offers a path to citizenship for illegal immigrants will simply encourage more people to illegally enter the United States. This was the case with the amnesty provided under the 1986 Immigration Reform and Control Act. Although the illegal population declined shortly after the legislation came into effect, it increased dramatically during the late 1980s and 1990s.

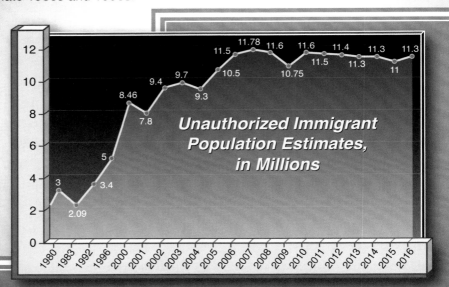

Unauthorized Immigrant Population Estimates, in Millions

Source: Procon.org, "Illegal Immigration, Population Estimates in the United States, 1969–2016." https://immigration.procon.org.

immigrants to apply for legal resident status and eventually to apply for US citizenship.

In the short term, conferring legal status on those immigrants already living in the country without documentation would certainly reduce the population of illegal aliens. But amnesty also sends the message that there is no punishment for those who break the rules. This is highly likely to encourage millions of other foreigners to try to enter the country illegally. Those who do so are likely to believe they will one day gain legal status through a future amnesty program.

The United States has offered amnesty to illegal immigrants before. In 1986 the Immigration Reform and Control Act (IRCA) provided a ten-year window in which illegal immigrants who had been living in the country prior to 1982 could apply for legal resident status. At the time, there were about 3.2 million illegal immigrants living in the United States. Over 2.7 million of these immigrants enrolled in the amnesty program before it expired, becoming eligible for eventual citizenship.

The IRCA also required the federal government to crack down on employers who hired illegal workers and to increase border security to prevent illegal crossings. However, the border and workplace restrictions were not strictly implemented or enforced by the administrations of George H.W. Bush (1989–1993) and Bill Clinton (1993–2001). As a result, during the 1990s the illegal immigrant population rose even faster than it had prior to the IRCA. The number of illegal immigrants reached 3.5 million by 1990, 5.7 million by 1995, and 8.6 million by 2000. It has continued to rise, and today the total number of illegal immigrants has stabilized at around 11.3 million. "People on all sides of the immigration argument agree that the 1986 Reform Act was a failure," notes journalist Dan Moffett. "It didn't keep illegal workers out of the workplace, it didn't deal with at least 2 million undocumented immigrants who ignored the law or were ineligible to come forward, and most of all, it didn't stop the flow of illegal immigrants into the country."[37]

> "[The 1986 Immigration Reform Act] didn't keep illegal workers out of the workplace, it didn't deal with at least 2 million undocumented immigrants who ignored the law or were ineligible to come forward, and most of all, it didn't stop the flow of illegal immigrants into the country."[37]
>
> —Journalist Dan Moffett

Existing Laws Must Be Enforced

Despite the failure of the IRCA to accomplish what Congress intended, the legislative formula of coupling amnesty with the promise of increased border security and workplace enforcement has been proposed numerous times since then to solve the problem of illegal immigration. Measures proposed in 2006, 2007, 2013, and 2018 have all failed to be enacted by Congress, largely because of concerns that they would not provide a permanent solution.

Perhaps the best approach would involve addressing the border security and workplace aspects first, making it harder for illegal immigrants to live in the United States, before considering any amnesty proposal. Requiring all employers to use the E-Verify system would close the loophole that lets companies get away with hiring undocumented workers. If these immigrants are not able to find a job, there would be little reason to remain in the United States. "Over time," notes William W. Chip of the Center for Immigration Studies, "most unauthorized aliens would find it so difficult to secure and retain employment that, like temporary legal workers whose visas have expired, they would quietly return home."[38]

> "Over time, most unauthorized aliens would find it so difficult to secure and retain employment that, like temporary legal workers whose visas have expired, they would quietly return home."[38]
>
> —William W. Chip, Center for Immigration Studies

Increased border security is important, but over the past decade most of the undocumented came here legally and then overstayed the terms of their visas. A system must be developed to more carefully monitor temporary workers and visitors, and a process must be implemented to immediately remove those who try to stay beyond their legal term.

Legal Status, but Not Citizenship

Once those systems are in place and functioning properly, it might be appropriate to look into a limited amnesty for some illegal immigrants, such as the Dreamers. One option would be to offer them a path to legal resident status without the possibility of full US citizenship.

Under this approach, the Dreamers could never enjoy all the rights and benefits of US citizens. That is the penalty for breaking the rules. As *National Affairs* writer Peter Skerry points out, this status will affect only the Dreamers themselves. Their descendants would have citizenship status by virtue of their birth on US soil. Skerry writes:

> Permanent non-citizen status would be inferior to naturalization and full citizenship. . . . But it is also worth emphasizing that the force and stigma of this penalty would be strongest at the outset, and would fade over time as those on whom it would be imposed aged and eventually passed away. And if we committed seriously to stemming subsequent illegal immigration, then any stigma attaching to beneficiaries of this proposal would further dissipate over time.[39]

The status of noncitizen national already exists in American Samoa, an unincorporated territory of the United States located in the south Pacific Ocean. Residents of American Samoa can travel freely into and out of the United States, are permitted to live and work within the United States without restrictions, and are entitled to US passports. Yet they are not citizens and may not vote in state or federal elections.

Every year, the United States grants permanent legal resident status to about 1 million immigrants, providing them with a clear path to US citizenship. That is more than all the rest of the nations of the world combined. Our immigration system is fair and reflects American values. Granting the benefit of citizenship to those who knowingly broke the rules would be unfair to all the foreign-born individuals who came to America legally.

Source Notes

Overview: Illegal Immigration

1. Robert Warren and Donald Kerwin, "The 2,000 Mile Wall in Search of a Purpose," Center for Migration Studies, 2018. http://cmsny.org.

Chapter One: Does Illegal Immigration Hurt US Workers?

2. Donald Trump, "Remarks by President Trump in State of the Union Address," White House, January 30, 2018. www.whitehouse.gov.
3. Adam Davidson, "Do Illegal Immigrants Actually Hurt the US Economy?," *New York Times Magazine*, February 17, 2013. www.nytimes.com.
4. Beth Healy and Megan Woolhouse, "In Building Boom, Immigrant Workers Face Exploitation," *Boston Globe*, September 18, 2016. www.boston globe.com.
5. Robert Rector, "Reducing Illegal Immigration Through Employment Verification, Enforcement, and Protection," Heritage Foundation, October 7, 2008. www.heritage.org.
6. Quoted in Tatiana Sanchez, "E-Verify Doesn't Prevent Many Companies from Hiring Undocumented Workers," *San Jose (CA) Mercury News*, January 20, 2018. www.mercurynews.com.
7. Quoted in Natalie Kitroeff and Geoffrey Mohan, "Wages Rise on California Farms. Americans Still Don't Want the Job," *Los Angeles Times*, March 17, 2017. www.latimes.com.
8. Michael A. Clemens, *International Harvest: A Case Study of How Foreign Workers Help American Farms Grow Crops—and the Economy*. New York: Partnership for a New American Economy and the Center for Global Development, 2013. www.newamericaneconomy.org.
9. Quoted in Mark Engler, "Immigration Economics: An Interview with Professor Giovanni Peri," Foreign Policy in Focus, September 16, 2018. www.afsc.org.
10. Noah Smith, "Immigrants Haven't Hurt Pay for Americans," Bloomberg, February 14, 2018. www.bloomberg.com.

Chapter Two: Does Illegal Immigration Strain Public Services?

11. Quoted in Michelle Ye Hee Lee, "Trump's False Claim That Undocumented Immigrants Collect Social Security Benefits," *Washington Post*, August 20, 2016. www.washingtonpost.com.

12. Robert A. Stribley, "No, Undocumented Immigrants Aren't Stealing Your Benefits," *Huffington Post*, November 21, 2017. www.huffingtonpost.com.
13. US Chamber of Commerce, "Immigration Myths and Facts," 2013. www.uschamber.com.
14. Lisa Christensen Gee et al., "Undocumented Immigrants State and Local Tax Contribution," Institute on Taxation and Economic Policy, March 2017. https://itep.org.
15. Stephen Goss et al., "Effects of Unauthorized Immigration on the Actuarial Status of the Social Security Trust Funds," Social Security Administration, 2013. www.ssa.gov.
16. Quoted in Molly Redden, "Undocumented Immigrants Avoid Vital Nutrition Services for Fear of Deportation," *Guardian* (Manchester), May 9, 2017. www.theguardian.com.
17. Matthew O'Brien et al., "The Fiscal Burden of Illegal Immigration on United States Taxpayers," Federation for American Immigration Reform, September 27, 2017. www.fairus.org.

Chapter Three: Are Stronger Border Enforcement Measures Needed?

18. Quoted in US Department of Homeland Security, "DHS Statement on President Trump Visit to Border Wall Prototypes," press release, March 13, 2018. www.dhs.gov.
19. Quoted in Jeff Flake: US Senator–Arizona, "Committee Approves Flake-McCain-Johnson Boots on the Border Act," press release, May 17, 2017. www.flake.senate.gov.
20. Nelson Balido, "Technology Will Be a Critical Component of a Good Border Wall," *Hill* (Washington, DC), October 14, 2017. http://thehill.com.
21. Balido, "Technology Will Be a Critical Component of a Good Border Wall."
22. Quoted in Chantal da Silva, "US Border Under Siege, Says Trump, and Mexico Is Doing Nothing About It," *Newsweek*, May 4, 2018. www.newsweek.com.
23. Quoted in Priscilla Alvarez, "What's Next for Trump's Border Wall?," *Atlantic*, March 16, 2018. www.theatlantic.com.
24. Quoted in Nolan D. McCaskill, "Trump Promises Wall and Massive Deportation Program," *Politico*, August 31, 2016. www.politico.com.
25. David Bier, "Why the Wall Won't Work," *Reason*, May 2017. http://reason.com.
26. Frank Newport, "Building a Wall out of Sync with American Public Opinion," Gallup, April 27, 2017. https://news.gallup.com.

27. Robert Warren and Donald Kerwin, "The 2,000 Mile Wall in Search of a Purpose: Since 2007 Visa Overstays Have Outnumbered Undocumented Border Crossers by a Half Million," *Journal on Migration and Human Security*, 2017. http://jmhs.cmsny.org.
28. Quoted in Ashish Kumar Sen, "Halting the 'Caravans': Addressing Push Factors Is Key to Stemming Flow of Unauthorized Migrants, Says Atlantic Council's Jason Marczak," *New Atlanticist* (blog), Atlantic Council, April 3, 2018. www.atlanticcouncil.org.
29. Mark L. Schneider, "We Don't Need a Wall to Manage Migration from Mexico," *Miami Herald*, February 3, 2017. www.miamiherald.com.

Chapter Four: Should Illegal Immigrants Be Given a Path to Citizenship?

30. Quoted in Frank Newport, "Americans Oppose Border Walls, Favor Dealing with DACA," Gallup, June 20, 2018. https://news.gallup.com.
31. Quoted in Jill Colvin and Andrew Taylor, "Trump Open to Letting Dreamers 'Morph into' Citizens," *U.S. News & World Report*, January 24, 2018. www.usnews.com.
32. Victoria Balara, "Fox News Poll: 83 Percent Support Pathway to Citizenship for Illegal Immigrants," Fox News, September 28, 2017. www.foxnews.com.
33. Francesc Ortega et al., "The Economic Benefits of Passing the Dream Act," Center for American Progress, September 18, 2017. www.americanprogress.org.
34. Robert Lynch and Patrick Oakford, "The Economic Effects of Granting Legal Status and Citizenship to Undocumented Immigrants," Center for American Progress, March 20, 2013. www.americanprogress.org.
35. Ben Gitis and Laura Collins, "The Budgetary and Economic Costs of Addressing Unauthorized Immigration: Alternative Strategies," American Action Forum, March 6, 2015. www.americanactionforum.org.
36. Barack Obama, "Remarks by the President in Address to the Nation on Immigration," White House, November 20, 2014. https://obamawhitehouse.archives.gov.
37. Dan Moffett, "What Is the Immigration Reform and Control Act of 1986?," ThoughtCo., June 14, 2018. www.thoughtco.com.
38. William W. Chip, "Mass Deportations vs. Mass Legalization: A False Choice," Center for Immigration Studies, March 21, 2017. https://cis.org.
39. Peter Skerry, "Splitting the Difference on Illegal Immigration," *National Affairs*, Winter 2013. www.nationalaffairs.com.

Illegal Immigration Facts

Illegal Immigrants in the Workforce

- About 8 million illegal immigrants have jobs in the United States, according to a 2016 study by the Pew Research Center. They make up about 5 percent of the US labor force.
- According to the US Department of Agriculture, illegal immigrants make up 26 percent of the workers in farming/agricultural occupations. US-born workers make up 54 percent of the farming workforce, and legal immigrants make up 20 percent.
- Illegal immigrants make up about 15 percent of the workers in construction occupations. The Pew Research Center reports that in 2014, more than 25 percent of all drywall installers, roofers, construction painters, and brick masons were illegal immigrants.
- Statistics from the US Department of Labor show that in 2017, foreign-born workers over age twenty-five without a high school diploma earned $506 per week, on average. By comparison, native-born workers without a high school degree earned $560 per week.
- The Congressional Budget Office estimates that 30 to 50 percent of undocumented workers do not report their income by filing federal tax returns. This means they are not paying federal or state income taxes.

Border Enforcement

- The US-Mexico border runs about 2,000 miles (3,219 km) from the Pacific Ocean to the Gulf of Mexico. There are fences or other barriers on about one-third of the border. Most of this fencing was a result of the Secure Fence Act of 2006.
- There are forty-eight legal crossing points on the US-Mexico border. There are thirty-five border cities, and more than 12 million people live near the border.

- In the 2018 fiscal year (October 2017–September 2018), US Customs and Border Protection apprehended or detained nearly 400,000 people attempting to cross the southern border. That figure was higher than that in 2017 (303,916) and about the same as in 2016 (408,870).
- A 2017 report by the US Department of Homeland Security estimated that the security fence proposed by Donald Trump could cost nearly $22 billion to construct.
- A June 2018 Gallup Poll found that 57 percent of Americans oppose expanded construction of walls between the United States and Mexico. Forty-one percent of those who responded oppose additional border walls.
- In 2017 the Bureau of Justice Statistics reported that 50 percent of the 165,265 total arrests made during 2014 by federal authorities were for immigration-related offenses, such as crossing the border illegally or smuggling others into the United States. In 2004 immigration-related offenses accounted for 28 percent of all federal arrests.

DACA Recipients

- From 2012 to 2017, approximately 800,000 young illegal immigrants received work permits and protection from deportation through a federal government program known as Deferred Action for Childhood Arrivals (DACA).
- More than 94 percent of DACA recipients were born in Mexico, Central America, or South America. Mexico is the top country of origin for DACA recipients, followed by El Salvador, Guatemala, and Honduras.
- Forty-five percent of all DACA recipients live in California (29 percent) or Texas (16 percent). Illinois (5 percent), New York (5 percent), Florida (4 percent), and Arizona (4 percent) also have significant DACA populations.
- According to 2017 data from the US Citizenship and Immigration Services, 53 percent of DACA recipients are female, and 47 percent are male. The largest group of DACA recipients (37 percent) were age twenty-one to twenty-five. Eighty-three percent of DACA recipients

were single in 2017, 15 percent were married, and 1 percent were divorced.

- According to a June 2018 Gallup Poll, 83 percent of Americans support a proposal to allow immigrants who were brought to the United States illegally as children the chance to become US citizens if they meet certain requirements over a period of time.

Illegal Immigrant Population

- Under a program called Temporary Protected Status (TPS), more than 320,000 immigrants from ten nations were permitted to live and work in the United States, because it was too dangerous for them to return to their home countries. Seventy-six percent of TPS recipients were from El Salvador, Haiti, Nicaragua, or Sudan.
- The Temporary Protected Status program did not grant permanent legal resident status to immigrants, but, like DACA, it protected those enrolled from deportation. The Trump administration announced it did not intend to renew TPS after 2018.
- Since 2009 there has been a surge in the number of unaccompanied alien children (UACs) at the US-Mexico border. These are foreigners under age eighteen who are not accompanied by a parent or legal guardian but seek entrance to the United States.
- In 2017 the Office of Refugee Resettlement cared for 40,810 UACs. Ninety-five percent of those who came to the US border in 2017 were from the Northern Triangle region of Central America: 45 percent from Guatemala, 27 percent from El Salvador, and 23 percent from Honduras.
- About 68 percent of all UACs are boys.
- A February 2018 study by the Cato Institute found that illegal immigrants were 25 percent less likely to be convicted of homicide than native-born Americans.

Related Organizations and Websites

American Immigration Council
1331 G St. NW, Suite 200
Washington, DC 20005
e-mail: wfeliz@immcouncil.org
website: www.immigrationpolicy.org

The American Immigration Council is a nonprofit organization that promotes laws, policies, and attitudes that honor the United States' proud history as a nation of immigrants. It attempts to provide policy makers and the general public with access to accurate information about the effects of immigration on the US economy and society.

Center for Immigration Studies
1629 K St. NW, Suite 600
Washington, DC 20006
website: www.cis.org

The Center for Immigration Studies is public policy organization devoted to research on and analysis of the impact of immigration on the United States. It advocates lower levels of immigration and a warmer welcome for those who are admitted.

Federation for American Immigration Reform (FAIR)
25 Massachusetts Ave. NW, Suite 330
Washington, DC 20001
e-mail: dray@fairus.org
website: www.fairus.org

FAIR is a public interest organization that supports stricter border management, lower levels of overall immigration, and a greater focus on attracting highly skilled immigrants.

Migration Policy Institute

1400 Sixteenth St. NW, Suite 300
Washington, DC 20036
e-mail: info@migrationpolicy.org
website: www.migrationpolicy.org

The Migration Policy Institute is an independent, nonpartisan think tank dedicated to analysis of the movement of people worldwide. The institute publishes books, reports, fact sheets, and the online journal *Migration Information Source*.

National Immigration Forum

50 F St. NW, Suite 300
Washington, DC 20001
website: www.immigrationforum.org

Founded in 1982, the National Immigration Forum advocates for the value of immigrants and immigration to our nation. The forum supports responsible federal immigration policies that address current economic and national security needs while also honoring the ideal of America as a land of opportunity.

National Network for Immigrant and Refugee Rights

310 Eighth St., Suite 310
Oakland, CA 94607
e-mail: nnirrinfo@nnirr.org
website: www.nnirr.org

The goal of the National Network for Immigrant and Refugee Rights is to promote a fair immigration and refugee policy in the United States and to defend and expand the rights of all immigrants and refugees, regardless of immigration status.

Pew Hispanic Center

1615 L St. NW, Suite 800
Washington, DC 20036
website: www.pewhispanic.org

The Pew Hispanic Center is a nonpartisan research organization that seeks to improve understanding of the US Hispanic population. It conducts research and public opinion surveys on various social, economic, and political topics involving Latinos in the United States.

UnidosUS

1126 Sixteenth St. NW, Suite 600
Washington, DC 20036
website: www.unidosus.org

UnidosUS is the nation's largest Latino civil rights and advocacy organization. The organization was founded in 1968 as the National Council of La Raza.

For Further Research

Books

Dale Hanson Bourke, *Immigration: Tough Questions, Direct Answers.* Downers Grove, IL: InterVarsity, 2014.

Aviva Chomsky, *Undocumented: How Immigration Became Illegal.* Boston: Beacon, 2014.

Tom Gjelten, *A Nation of Nations: A Great American Immigration Story.* New York: Simon and Schuster, 2015.

David M. Haugen, *Human Rights in Focus: Illegal Immigrants.* San Diego, CA: ReferencePoint Press, 2017.

David M. Haugen, *What Should Be Done About Illegal Immigration?* San Diego, CA: ReferencePoint Press, 2017.

Noel Merino, *Illegal Immigration.* Farmington Hills, MI: Greenhaven, 2015.

John Moore, *Undocumented: Immigration and the Militarization of the United States–Mexico Border.* New York: Powerhouse, 2018.

Rick Schmerhorn, *Undocumented Immigrants and Homeland Security.* Philadelphia: Mason Crest, 2017.

Internet Sources

Mary Jo Dudley, "These US Industries Can't Work Without Illegal Immigrants," CBS News, June 25, 2018. www.cbsnews.com/news/illegal-immigrants-us-economy-farm-workers-taxes.

David Inserra, "Dreaming of Amnesty: Legalization Will Spur More Illegal Immigration," Heritage Foundation, October 30, 2017. www.heritage.org/immigration/report/dreaming-amnesty-legalization-will-spur-more-illegal-immigration.

Jerry Kammer, "Three Decades of Failed Reform: Immigration Politics and the Collapse of Worksite Enforcement," Center for Immigration Studies, August 2, 2018. https://cis.org/Oped/Three-Decades-Failed-Reform-Immigration-Politics-and-Collapse-Worksite-Enforcement.

Fred Lucas, "What Trump Could Learn from the Reagan Immigration Amnesty," Daily Signal, October 8, 2017. www.dailysignal.com/2017/10/08/what-trump-could-learn-from-the-reagan-immigration-amnesty.

Jeffrey Miron, "Forget the Wall Already, It's Time for the US to Have Open Borders," Cato Institute, July 31, 2018. www.cato.org/publications/commentary/forget-wall-already-its-time-us-have-open-borders.

Alicia Sasser Modestino, "Why Trump's Deportation Plan Could Damage the Economy," News@Northeastern, March 1, 2017. https://news.northeastern.edu/2017/03/01/how-trumps-deportation-plan-could-damage-the-economy.

Robert Siegel and Selena Simons-Duffin, "How Did We Get to 11 Million Unauthorized Immigrants?," *All Things Considered*, National Public Radio, March 7, 2017. www.npr.org/2017/03/07/518201210/how-did-we-get-to-11-million-unauthorized-immigrants.

Alex Tyson, "Public Backs Legal Status for Immigrants Brought to US Illegally as Children, but Not a Bigger Border Wall," Pew Research Center, January 19, 2018. www.pewresearch.org/fact-tank/2018/01/19/public-backs-legal-status-for-immigrants-brought-to-u-s-illegally-as-children-but-not-a-bigger-border-wall.

USA Today Network, "The Wall: Unknown Stories, Unintended Consequences," *USA Today*, 2018. www.usatoday.com/border-wall.

Index

About the Author

Jim Gallagher is the author of more than twenty books for young adults. His books, written for various publishers, include *The Johnstown Flood*, *Causes of the Iraq War*, and *A Girl's/Guy's Guide to Conflict*. He lives in central New Jersey with his wife, LaNelle, and their three children.